FAULT LINES

ALSO BY KENDEL HIPPOLYTE

Island in the Sun, Side Two...
Bearings
Labyrinth
Birthright
Night Vision

ACKNOWLEDGEMENTS

Many thanks to the following journals and anthologies in which some of these poems have appeared:

Caribbean Review of Books: 'Poet 003'
BIM: 'Mack 1', 'Mack 2', 'Really'
Callaloo: 'Going'
So Much Things To Say: 'Reggae Rant'
Sixty Poems For Haiti: 'Slash Bargain'
Bermuda Anthology of Poetry, Vol 2: 'Village'

KENDEL HIPPOLYTE

FAULT LINES

PEEPAL TREE

First published in Great Britain in 2012
Peepal Tree Press Ltd
17 King's Avenue
Leeds LS6 1QS
UK

ISBN 13: 9781845231941

Supported by
ARTS COUNCIL
ENGLAND

CONTENTS

WINDOWS

Do people still look out of windows?
When i was growing up, it seemed
that was where some people lived.
Ma Fred, Mister Fred, Miss Lala, there were others…
Some adults were just heads in windows, forearms on windowsills,
eyes that looked at us   then   beyond.
Their house interiors receded into mystery behind them,
a coloured dimness exactly right for being at home in.

They are receding now –
Ma Fred, Mister Fred, Miss Lala and the others –
into paintings and ideas for paintings,
into Wednesday afternoons when midweek was the half-day,
walls mottling the light, leaf-shadow on the paling fences, even the asphalt
seeming to hold not too much heat or too many cars
so dogs would lie down in the street and yawn,
get up in their own time and slouch away
as vehicles moved at the same pace as the afternoon
till they, along with everything, turned a sharp corner, left,
out of the deceptive lull of the mid-twentieth century
before all this.

They are becoming paintings –
Ma Fred, Mister Fred, Miss Lala and the others
resting at windowsills, looking out of their windows
at the dogs, the cars, at a child following his fore-shadow
at something else beyond   looking
– we have come to realize – at us now.
Composed, within their windows,
they are paintings that we frame, gilt-edged, in light
of all that we have come to since.

GOING

Along the Sunday morning road, west coast, uphill from Canaries to Soufriere,
my son asks from the backseat: "Daddy, where are we?"
And, reaching to pluck a name and finding none, i slip,
falling into a crevasse, the meaning of the question, the meaning
of my not having an answer, rushing upward past me
as i clutch at blurred-green-bush-brown-rock, not grasping anything.
Approaching Soufriere, i wonder: Suppose i had been able to say
"Belvedere" or "Bouton" or – what then? He'd have said "Oh"
and then most probably, "How far is it to Soufriere?"
In the intuitive logic of a child, where you are going
tells you where you are.
i think of answers others might have given to his question:
"We're in an area of prime real estate."
"Da is where my grandfather planted tangerines."
"The Kalinago had a settlement here three hundred years ago."
True. But in his logic, where are we?
Entering town, an old man, sitting in his doorway as we drive past, chewing meditatively,
shifts the question to another corner of his mouth;
a lanky youth, a black branch snapped in a sudden wind,
just up ahead, gusting across the narrow street, scuds closer,
the question a belligerent rasp of sandals on hot asphalt.
If my son asked now "Where are we?", i'd say: "In Soufriere, passing the church."
Sunday morning, the scent of Vaseline and talcum powder, an incense offering;
children, their foreheads shining, delicate dark collarbones fragrantly dusted white, always;
boys awkward in new shoes, long-sleeved shirts, girls dressed like birthday cakes;
the glistening of pink and yellow taffeta rustling in Sunday light around the church.
On the level grey stretch of road now before The Still, i can almost forget
the sudden vertiginous mindfall that my son's question had dislodged me into.
Then at the last curve – not quite a corner, too gentle – we pass an elderly lady,
someone of my mother's age, waiting at the road's edge for a van.
We pass so close that i could touch her – though, not really. She is unreachable.
In the peach organdie and poplin, lace-trimmed, scallop-collared fussy graciousness
        of her church dress,
    hand-millinered hat, white purse, white block-heeled shoes, gold earrings and gold
        brooch to match,

she is standing in another time. She is standing
in the middle of the last century of the old millennium in Saint Lucia
when the mass was still intoned in Latin and all the priests spoke French.
She is waiting to go to church. But, in truth, in this moment held above us
      like a communion wafer,
the church, the square, the streets, the town are waiting, in a kind of offertory, for her.
When she enters the church, all will settle into place and know where they are.
She is going, leaving me the now augmented burden of my young son's question.
When she goes, she will take the green curve of the roadside with her,
the "Bonjou, tout moun" as she enters the van, the Sunday morning light
and before we know it, night will come.

AULD LANG SYNE

A beachside restaurant, Old Year's Night,
the locals sandwiched between the tourists and expatriates,
each table a tossed salad of conversation pickled with accents,
the seasoned tabletalk just an accompaniment to the jazz combo;
an occasional silence poured a mixed dressing on the whole thing.
We should have sung – for old times, auld acquaintance,
for old flames finally left unattended, for last bows,
we should have sung for the decembering of our lives,
we should have sung for Christ's sake.
We didn't. Our mouths, if nothing else, were full; we ate
the year's last meal, which we would pay for later.
About ten to the hour, the champagne bubbled round.
We fizzed as well, expecting something.
We got fireworks.
We stood, sat, leaned, grouped ourselves awkwardly
together on the last day of the year, looking toward the firmament,
proclaiming "Ooo", "Aaah", "Oh", without awe,
without seeing   through the razzledazzling incandescence
a black sky beyond.

VILLAGE

The village that the minivan was travelling to was vanishing
as we drove. Somewhere in ourselves we knew that.
It might have even been the reason finally for the driver speeding.

Along the way, roadwork gangs worked in the punishing
heat and dust and noise and smell of progress toward what-
ever it was that progress was supposed to be leading

us toward – not the village, which, as it grew larger, was diminishing.
The dust! It was phantasmagorical how it could suddenly blot
bits of the landscape out, trees wavering briefly and receding

into a grey haze of vehicles-men-vegetation merged in an undistinguishing
slow-motion flurry. As we drove into it, we drew the windows shut
as though the dust and haze were all outside us. The driver revved, exceeding –

if there was one – our limit. And as we hurried through that spirit-famishing
landscape, i was wondering: What drove him? Drove us? And what
precisely in the village, beyond our normal businesses, were we really needing?

Because we did not find it. Whatever drove us was also banishing
what we were driven to. When we arrived, in truth, the village was not
there. Perhaps the arterial road we'd followed was misleading.

The village that the minivan was travelling to was vanishing
as we drove to somewhere in our selves. We knew. And that
might have been why we drove there with a sense of desperation, pleading.

A PLACE

Alright, someone from Europe might not call it a city.
But if a city mean a place
where ground so hard people stop bury navel string,
and no one looking at a tree can say:
"Is my grandfather plant that"; a place
where, no matter how much street lamp light,
all you look out for, all you see, are shadows; a place
where, days and days and days, you only
seeing people you eh really know;
and you already starting to accept, believe
that's how it is, that's how life go –
well, if a city is a place just so,
then this plenty-shack-with-couple-condo/jalopy-SUV/spendfast-payslow/
so-it-come-so-it-go/quick-dead/continual-state-of-inbetween-uncertainty
is, in some sort of way, i guess, perhaps
        a city

PARADISE

Every time this tourist ship name *Paradise* come dock in the harbour
you does realize we never going to make it.
Because the tallest building in the town – and is a big-ass bank –
still down below the level of the high regard of Grade X tourists with sunglasses
watching from behind the super-duper plexi-glass windows of the upper deck,
tinted so it hard to see through them, flashing like mirrors in the Caribbean light,
and all the surrounding hills and houses in them looking so damn small;
the super-duper sunglasses watching, looking down on bank, on busy main street,
on people scurrying up and down as if they have to do their business fast
before the good ship *Paradise* leave – again.
And the ambition of each government, whether right or left behind,
is to build something higher than the smokestacks of this luxury limer
lounging all day in the harbour, dribbling vanilla-strawberry tourists, slurping them back up,
then sliding off again like an absentee owner, come to make a quick cheque on things
before he gone again, puffing smoke and flashing winking mirrors.
Paradise – going elsewhere,
gone.

8:30, store about to open, SALE, crowd at his back

shoved. Suddenly, in front of him – *In front? How come? He thought he was*
first in the pack – a man, looking exactly like him, dressed like him,

but going the other way, against the crowd, coming toward him, coming to himself,

rushed at him, one arm raised. *In warning? In attack?*

Not sure. His own arm, he just realized, was up.

Then the shining glass of the show window smashed,

the sudden man shattered into bright, jagged fragments and then vanished,

and he, down on the sidewalk now, watching his clothes changing their colour,

looked up, trying to see through the crowd, to find where he, the man, had gone.

Around him, everything – household furniture, appliances, people and banners
      shouting SALE –

loosened and fell into each other, into a red blur

that dimmed briefly when he wavered upright,

brightening when he began to run, racing ahead

of his own scattering blood till he reached the health centre.

All the wailing journey to the hospital, he saw the man, his twin,

outside the ambulance, looking back at him through the glass window, whispering:

The price. The price. The price. Tell me the price.

FAULT LINES

The lines appear on sidewalks and on streets just recently resurfaced,
on bridges and on buildings, the creases, cracks, accumulating;
the fractures of a thin, brittle civilization aging prematurely.
The hand of something dying scrabbles these last messages everywhere,
a harsh cuneiform trying to break through surfaces into our understanding.
But we can barely read that ancient language now, of earth writing itself.
We walk between the lines, fill in the blank telling cracks, deconstruct, if need be,
our crumbling edifices breaking out in fault lines from trying to contain what we've become.
The hand is writing too on faces – lines of bewilderment, fear, guilt;
other unfinished lines trail off, coagulating red on bodies left as messages,
torsos punctuated with the exclamation marks of knife wounds, full stops of bullet holes;
final sentences marked on faces of those who used to be too young to kill or to be killed.
Something is desperately writing a threnodic poem to us, hoping we will read
the lines appearing on the sidewalks, streets, bridges, buildings, bodies, faces. But
we do not read – and what hope for a poem, like this one, struggling to translate,
with nothing but words, these dark fault lines of our disintegration into poetry?

MS

Searching – but not deep enough – for an original, forgotten scroll, instead
i found a manuscript, in gradually deteriorating cursive, in a discoloured notebook,
a history of the twentieth century, traced in the florid blue lines of the superior rich
style of an ancien regime, its characters dwindling down blemished, once-white surfaces,
with dark scrawled questions, insults, curses, crowded in margins like the poor:
page after page, the contradictory elegantly sprawled/angrily penned mess-
age of a world divided to the right and left along a fading red fault line.

KRAKEN

The bloated ghostly kraken that has gripped the globe for centuries
is failing fast, disgorging its glut all over us, thrashing in spasms
as its tentacles, more numerous and illusional than lines of longitude, flail desperately
in the thick, hot, noxious air that it exhausts itself in, lashing at itself
while it still grips the world, issuing the spectral poison that has seeped
from its suckering skin into ourselves for so long that we never felt our own paralysis
till now, as the long green kraken with the coined eyes embraces us more closely
and we hope that these are not its throes of death which we are feeling now.

THE AGE OF DINOSAURS

Lands quake in the boom of their approach, their hulked conglomerated mass
unstoppable. Blunt, blundering, aggregated deadening weight, a bludgeoning tread,
billions of pounds, a bullish corporate bulk hungering through all places.

Above, the ripped shredded clouds, the scraped bruised heads of mountains
show they have passed there too. Their droppings, where they fall, blight
unto desert and vast tundra of clenched fragments dying, the left tares of violence.

Gnashed by metal teeth to strips, the forests blister in a sick light.
Sounds of grind and snarling, screech, the ratcheting click of unsheathed claws.
The gored earth bleeds black, flesh of hills and valleys flayed bone-white.

And small things quake. They shiver, shrink smaller still;
they starve down to lean skin and bright hot eyes watching
lives graded down to morsels, sputum, the effluent waste of giants.

It is the age of dinosaurs. They come from the deep places,
the neon fluorescent caves of Hav, the ultra-violent bunkers of Gov
and their hunger, if they would only know, is for eternity.

But in their massive ignorance they must gorge, growing immense, gross, wanting
always to fill themselves into the always widening spaces of their caves, their bunkers
where they return each night and feel so small, so lost, they rush out, ravening.

MACK 1

What he's most wanting is not what he wants
Is not what he craves
Deeper than avarice, if he'd let himself feel, is the haunting hunger
That saves

He holds the whole world with his hired hands
Desperately trying
To have it. But trapped in his spasming grip, his seizures, the earth
Is dying

He cannot stop grasping. Whatever he sees
He is accounting
Its self into cost into price into sale into profit into himself
McWanting

He gluts till he's wracked with a spasm and spews
Blood-flecked bits of self
A wasting consumption leaving him gasping for life and clutching
At pelf

What is the deep whole he's wanting to fill?
For what is he hungry?
Gorged with the planet's green flesh, its black bile, its ripped out entrails
And yet empty

Running to every thing and running everything
Avoiding the whole
He's afraid that will swallow him into its void where he has no thing
No soul

And yet he touches us, Midas-like, desperately
Haunted and haunting
And we, his children, we bear his name like a watermark, secretly
McWanting

The flowers of McKallus grow everywhere
Sahara to Arctic, skyscraper to shack
On each one he ravishes personal care
Rapt, necrophiliac

He cultivates thousands in each killing field
He sows landmines that bloom in bursts of dead petals
Black tulips of shrapnel, poppies of congealed
Burned-flesh-and-metals

From the cut stalks of limbs, hacked crinums of hands,
Picked fading irises, he makes a bouquet
Corsages of flesh wounds are what he demands
New blows each day

In his sedulous experimental plots of malevolence
Nyarabuye, Columbine, the gardens of bane
He plucks, from a dark loam of pleasure and violence,
The lilies of pain

The sick-sweet scent of the flowers of cruelty
Intrigue him intensely. Sometimes he grows,
With cigarette burns on the face of a baby,
A delicate rose

Crumpled leaves of petitions, a guard's flytrap grin
A hand-out extended toward you, acanthous
Surreal, the subtle forms of phytoxin
Of flowers of McKallus

His seeds germinate in a subsoul of mystery
Then burst through the surface, and we recognise
McKallus' bright efflorescence of cruelty
His blooms in our eyes

Old McNulland has a farm
So high, so wide, so low
It's everywhere and everyone
It spreads from yes to no

Acres of holes the colour of nothing
Boundaries of null, a void unending
Stretching past where the i can see
A harvest of silence, hectares of empty

Old McNulland has a farm
So high, so dry, so no

Crops with no colour or shape or smell
Grow everywhere but it's hard to tell
Livestock, raised for your milk and meat
But you must look inside-out to see it

Old McNulland has a farm
So sly, so snide, so low

Who eats the crops, who slaughters the beasts?
Who presides over the ghoulish feasts?
And when it has eaten, what is its shit?
What do you name lives with no meaning or spirit?

Old McNulland has a farm
No I, so lie, so woe

Lives on conveyer belts run without reaching
A sense of existence continuously leaching
Neon spectres in daytime that bleach in the light
An emptiness forevering out into white

Old McNulland has a farm
Beyond the I, row after row
Every where and every one
We die, no why, just so

THE BALEFIRES OF LONDON (AFTER BLAKE…)

I.

The sons and daughters of Hav rave in the streets.
They make pyres of imposing establishments, low corner shops and quietly parked cars.
A wounded building in Croydon howls in the agony of dying,
gouting flames out of its gutted orifices, spurting hot tears from gouged eyes.
The children of Hav roam like lava through the streets of London.

Blue phalanxes of Gov move uniformly in advancing ramparts,
shields, batons, bodies braced at the roving pyroclastic flow.
What is burning, what is turning into cinders, into ash
is more than edifices, more than their crammed commodities leering behind glass,
than greengrocers' fruit shrivelling into blackened stubs,
more than the age's metal and concrete and plastic integuments.
What is burning, which has no label and no barcoded price,
are the props and struts and beams of wall-eyed progress
which disintegrating civilizations must jerrybuild into their crumbling citizenry
to stave off the mind-shattering collapse into the madness of unmeaning.
The children of Hav rage fire, futile, against their cold and dark.

II.

The world-imperial duumvirate of Hav and Gov
early in the new millennium was buckling under the burden of itself,
all of its thiefdoms brittle, the tense truce between the deities splintering:
Hav, as Hav must, wanting more; Gov, the rationing ruler, measuring.
In Albion, between the clink of coins and rustling of commodities, a groaning:
as an overloaded goods truck grated downhill, braking against the threat
        of its momentum;
as a crane grundled another beam of Babel through the marred air above Tottenham;
as a hurtling train underground halted its harsh breath, disgorged, gorged, harried on.
A groaning. And, unseen, a fog roaming the city. Silver-grey. Their mingled emanation.

III

Your city, William Blake, warrior with your unsleeping sword of visionary corrosive light.
Sir, you who burned surfaces to reveal the inner body of reality in intaglio,
what would you have me see by the illumination of the balefires of London?
I follow your robust form, the vigorous unwavering line that marked your journey,
walking the path of heart's desire till I come, as all must, to the Gates of Wrath.
There, Hav's illegitimate children, consumed by a hungering they cannot slake with things,
bloated with slop, the hope of ever more, are gurging, ravenous for Eternity.
So in a seasonable summer when hot halogen lamps can almost burn away the dark,
Hav's unacknowledged bastards set fires unable to light or warm their deeper winter.
Afterward, his legal tender offspring, in the way of the well-manored, pronounce judgement
in sentences that unfold faultlessly to condemn the acts of damage and the damned.
The silver-grey substance of their deliberations issuing through tight-pursed lips
is the fuel that the fires fed on, an emanation softly precipitating now in words of ash
that cover almost everything, that settle on the damage and – although not quite – the damned.

IV.

Sir, I see – more clearly even as the flames mutter their last resentful curses,
as avid tongues lick helplessly at the left fragments, the least chunks of buildings –
how a consuming urge, beyond the reach of rationed satisfaction, might despair
and seek, in an ungovernable access, a Pyrrhiconoclastic consummation of itself.
To ash. Ash now. All, ash.
In the ruins an occasional eddying stirs a spectral dust, a fine aggregate compounded
of the tarnished coins of Hav, the crumbling grey stone blocks of Gov. Now visible
is the mingled emanation the citizens had always breathed, a miasma of the psyche, manifest.

V.

Mr. Blake, come walk again the chartered streets of London, you will see the marks
you saw more than two centuries ago. You will see and hear the milling of souls, crushed
between the grindstone and the quern of Hav and Gov, grain of the daily bread of giants.
You will see the poverty of affluence, the glut-and-retching of bulimic, self-blind Cyclopes.
The smell of ash, the drift of silver-grey existences will settle on your garments as you walk,

will pervade the skeletal burned-out husks and sift through the unscorched
       but strained facades
of long-standing family concerns and worthy enterprises. Fore-scent of the duumvirate's
       pyre. Ash.
Perhaps, prophet who walked across worlds seeking the Western Path, you may
       even see
an ember in the ash. If so, seer, poet, servitor of the Imagination, lift it above the scoria,
out of the futile consuming of itself, into the consummation offered by
       the engoldening blaze
of poetry, the fire that lasts, that makes even of burning buildings glowing
       illuminated manuscripts
that all may read and, reading in the fiery light of Los, may – as you, sir, always, did – see.

REGGAE RANT

(for Kamau Brathwaite)

Doom
> *!Scatter*

Doom
> *!Scatter*

Doom   **Doom**   **Doom**   **Doom**   **Doom**
> *!Scatter*   *!Scatter*   *!Scatter*   *!Scatter*

When the scrabbling city crawls nightways in penultimate light,
and the night wind is whorish, skirting around corners, twitching with a hiss down alleys,
the sound of the beast approaching
starts a backwash in the drains, stirs the unmoving muck in the canals which had
> begun as rivers

and crosses narrowing bridges crouched over our waste
to come to bodyslam us down, back down, onto the bass ground of our selves

Doom   **Doom**   **Doom**   **Doom**   **Doom**

claws strumming in a sweet, raking viciousness, eyelids down to the groin,
groin back again up to the eyelids

> *!Scatter*   *!Scatter*   *!Scatter*   *!Scatter*

Friday evening, the twilight, something wrings out dry the bleeding gauze-and-lint sky
> over us

flicking the drops of blood-flecked light in scattering gouts over the city,
over the heads of high school-kids starting to herd, to massive on the stomping grounds
> of corners,

and as the last drops of darklight fall spattering on their heads, a lowering swell
> of tongues babels upward,

an anti-Pentecostal unholy ghostly outpouring of jagged wordsong, infernal music
thud/*scratching*, **thud**/*scratching* on the hurriedly closing doors,
scoring the harsh truth of the Bosch's hell that we have made ourselves, that we
> now must live

Doom   Doom   Doom   Doom   Doom
   !Scatter   !Scatter   !Scatter   !Scatter

Where?
Hills cannot hide us, whiplashed by roads into near-nakedness
the scars of houses lurid in the rents of landscape

Doom
   !Scatter

Where?
No place a battering ram bass guitar won't breach

Doom
   !Scatter

Where?
No burglar bar, security fence, no chain, no cord
a one-drop slashing hand cannot chop through

Doom
   !Scatter

The downbeat beatdown dark tread sounding
deep into a stagnant-too-long ditch
a dread quaking, basal black reverberating doom, **doom**, **DOOM**
cracking the clagged surfaces of tepid lives that spew apart and scatter

   !Scatter   !Scatter …

But if, beyond this song, we listen –
what is it
that will – soon, soon – fall,
soon befall?
If we could squint up through the sludge that has become us,
if we could seer though the occluding scum, the self-colluding sly meniscus
cloying against the light searching our toxic depths,

if we could, through even one momentary mosaic crack of vision, see beyond –
what would it be, that brightening black dread
crescendoing from the cosmos down
to our end?

Doom   **Doom**   **Doom**   **Doom**   **Doom**
   !Scatter   *!Scatter*   *!Scatter*   *!Scatter*

Listen, the beast
is telling us, the heart-shocking beat
of its drop-dragging, maimed feet, *it-a-come*, approaching louder
is the rough overture of a tough, defensively offensive,
off-beat deliberately always
friend.

Doom
         !Scatter
                  Doom
                           !Scatter
                  Doom
                           !Scatter ...
                                    !Scatter...

                                             !Scatter...

What is the time?

It is the time of waiting

What time is it?

The time of little left

Is this the time?

It is the soon, the almost now

Tell me this time

The nearly now, the almost

What is this time?

The time of no more

Is our time – ?

No more, no more

i fill   the cup with water from the kitchen sink
you feel   that none of us reveres enough this gift
it falls   so clear, continuous, as though it always will
we fool   ourselves, forgetting its imperilled source
You foul   **the ancient rivers**, your voice warns, **and when**
they fail   **your glittering cup of drought will be fulfilled**

i lap	the last drops from my mug, turned downside up
you lip	your own, but pause, hearing a river, as
it lopes	too swiftly down, from source to end, because
we lop	the limbs and trunks of trees allaying it. It rales:
You loop	**your bridges, roads and cross me. Watch my tides now.**
They leap	**your levees, highways, surging in, to fill your cup.**

i reel	the line back in, expecting nothing; how long…?
you rale	spitting a blood-flecked phlegm at the grey river
it roils	wearily, dragging its sludge to a sick sea
we rail	– again – about big business. Wearily, you tell us:
You rile	***pointlessly. This is final. They're dying too.***
They rule	***a grey, ebbing empire. That line's empty.***

CONJUGATIONS – 4: NOX IRAE

i dim	the lamp, though night is rising round the house
you deem	my action fitting, dark calling to dark until
it dumbs	our very thoughts; the silence seeps in, spreading …
we dam	our rising fear as you, dispassionate, remind us:
You damn	***your greed too late; the levelling floods are here***
they doom	***us all on this last treeless, lightless night.***

i look	out where the sea, not far now, sips the shoreline in
you like	the still, stark beauty of this widening desolation
it lakes	the empty roadways, buildings, dissolving the idea of progress
we lack	all hope now. You tell us: ***This cannot be contained;***
you lock	***your dams, dykes, doors in vain; the waters rise;***
they lick	***unhurriedly at the diminishing world which they will swallow.***

LAST PHASE OF MOON

Sisters, earth and moon, daughters of the sun, and rivals.
The younger had been born autistic, her fire frozen to white light.
She watched the other one gyrating, flashing in her deciduous fashions;
watched earth in heat, in torrid writhing, show more skin;
watched, across millennia, the veils and tassels drop, her sister strip
while she herself wore simple shifts of white/black and she danced in silence.
Watchful always, eyes wide and full, or half-closed, or darkly narrowing, or shut,
she saw – and felt the knowledge shuddering through her: a new life would begin
after her sister stripped the last, scant tassel of her dance to death:
after the last felled tree shudders to earth, groaning a promise
that stirs the dust in whisperings over the dark side of moon.

THIS –

To name this seething emptiness perhaps would help
to fill it – though what it would be filled with,
what that name would be, the sound,
i cannot say. But it is this, just this –
the it, not just unsaid, but which, no matter how i wish,
cannot be said –

this

· is the emptiness.

IT IS EASY

One day, waking, you reach, you do not find
the reason

One day, out walking, you turn
a corner you have always missed

One day, at a gap in a sentence, a word
falls beyond sound, keeps falling

There are so many ways for it to happen
it is easy

In bed, devoid; round a bend; at a chasm in a sentence
looking down   listening   beyond sound

DANCE CRAZE

street after street
you see me dancing
traffic lock, is i moving
but what is my beat
tell me, what is my beat?

blocked there, you say
"What's he dancing to?"
but i dance only to you
whatever you play
whatunder you play

cause i hear things
in the sound clash of city
through this crazy polyphoney
all these weird voicings
a single voice sings

a sound that's not sound
through my feet to my head
i shake out the dread
i dance the unsound
dance to the unsound

SENTENCE

Today he was executed.
Not dragged against a wall,
running filth and spitting
prayers and obscenities
loud above the gunshouting.

Nothing like that.

He had been waiting
approximately forty years
for your considered verdict
on that first desperate appeal
which babies make.

A silence,
polite, urbane, suburban silence,
stopped the holes in his stomach,
stopped his crying
and later accompanied him from school
to gaol.

The no-thank-you
       can't-help-you
       wait-outside-please silence
well bred and softer than disease
had walked into his head.
He waited.

Today the silence sipped another drink
and asked him to explain
again.

By now the words were rusty,
meanings leaking out until
meaninglessness
became their truer meaning.

Today he heard
the space between
each word; and wondered…

The silence suddenly left his head
and, just as it exploded,
he fled inside,
hearing your crazed voices
on the final sentence.

THE SAYINGS OF API (THE CRAZY WHO NEVER SPEAKS) TO THE CITIZENS OF SANE

(for Shake Keane)

1.
Is all yuh in de land of Sane –
        I is not.
When you x-plain me,
        I has to disagree.
But then again,
        it eh me, is you
in Sane.

2.
Sane? I used to live there.
        Left. Too much dying,
festering, blood, pus.
        I saw it. "Mental" they said.
But fuh real, it was
        sanious.

3.
That famous Dane –
        might his problem be
that, like I, or even me,
        he could not remain
in Sane?

4.
Man, all dem i-lands –
        Sane Kitts, Sane Vincent, Sane Martin,
Sane Lucia (especially) –
        sane I crazy.

5.
The way I sees it, Sane
                is the superpower, not America.
An empire, far as i can see, spreading
                like a disease. All countries, people. Festering.
Sanies.

6.

Mornings, I rises early,
                mek a cool craze through the city,
and I gone before 8:00 a.m.
                That's when the sanes
go marching in.

7.
Day after day,
                dem caught in a net, in seine:
seine rise, sane set
                again. To pay
a living debt, dem earn
                the wages of Sane.

8.
And I see now
                the whole story:
all, all have saned,
                come short
of what should have been
                Glory.

REALLY

One of the city's madmen, a new one,
as the car eases past the traffic light,
takes rapid aim, fires, pumps, fires again –
a direct hit. The car
smashes the bridge broadside, half-spins, crashes
the other side, breaching the suddenly buckled girders, goes
right over, bonnet first, into the muddy, stinking river.

This is not what we see. We see
a lunatic gesticulating an exact mime of a shotgun murder.
Fantasy. A comic unreality where thoughts are triggering
blank acts that leave reality unharmed.
He is pathetic, that sniper into our world, his thoughts
ricochet off our rear windscreen back at him, he drops
out of our sight, diminishing in the mirror.

It's later, alone, i realise: i have been hit.
It shocks through me – the understanding, in a wondered moment,
that for him it was real, for where he really lives,
this happened. More, that where i – where we – live
is that same place.
For, considering what lies
between our thought and act, the dream/the life, where
do we live   truly?
If what touches, what we touch with, at the core,
is not, though it may seem that way, the act,
but the thoughtfelt intangible tip of what becomes the act;
if spirit not flesh, emotion not action, is our substance,
where else is there to live in truth
but in that place where he, the ineffectual murderer madman,
lived, when he fired dream-lethal thoughts at us, at what we felt
was our reality?

ATOM

There is a horror before the horror
of the heaven-high unholy pillar of cloud, skywide infernal flash, white fire,
skin-flesh-blood-bone-marrow vaporized into the timelessness of unimaginable unbeing,
the charred calligraphy of shadows scorched instantaneously onto the earth's parchment
and what had been thought a whole world shattering in the searing shock
of Hiroshima.
There is, before this horror, the horror insidious
of the moment of an original atom of humanity splitting,
the moment of one untrue man deliberately choosing
the self-blinding incandescence of the old glory of annihilation of the other.
And to know that moment, that horror, that Hiroshima,
the sundering of self i am imagining that has to be,
without shattering into centrifugal particles of the soul's disintegration,
i aim this poem from 31,500 scries above the inscrutable mindscape of that moment,
hoping my aim is right, hoping a searing bloom of white-hot light will burst up from
        that ground,
that falling cinders of words will singe into black ideograms of understanding that
        will remain
after the blinding revelation of that moment.

What was it, the moment of that choosing?
What was its sound, the smell of it, its taste and aftertaste?
How was it experienced?
As a bewildering misfiring of neurons fusillading across trenches of multiple synapses,
then an abrupt white silence?
Or something subtler?
A glimpsed fore-image of himself standing outside a cell door, looking through its
        grill window,
sliding it shut, sealing the other in, turning away?
Or – remembering what we know now of the banality of evil –
perhaps not even that?
Where in a true man could the moment of that choosing live?

If to be true is to be, somehow, one
thoughtfeelingaction a trinity unseparatable, the being of a sphere
without a faultline, with no divisive fissuring to intimate into itself disintegration,

44

then where in us, in truth, could all such moments live?
Nowhere.
They live where they must live, in the rifts of being,
in the clefts between O-riginal conscience and the self-fracturing act.
The atom of the true is indivisible.

But if, at what we thought was our atomic core, we are, already, a dividedness,
proton-neutron-scattering electrons of a selfhood barely held together in an
      unstable triad,
a shifting of alliances-and-enmities of thought-feeling-action in a shifting war-ceasefire-war
      without truce,
how can we be unembattled, how can we be one, how can we
piece together our selves unto the true, the lasting peace?
There is the horror, inside us,
of the chain reaction fissioning of lies that split lies into other lies that split lies
that implode the fragile selfhood, that perpetrate the daily, deadly devastations of our being
which are the necessary conditions of normality.

Yet nothing of all this absolves his act. Nothing dissolves the blood of innocents.
Even the corridors of war have doors you may not open,
entrances into the chambers of the infra-human that open only once, shut once
you have stepped through, locking yourself away for ever from the true.
What lives there lives in the softly irradiating silence of the other Hiroshima.

i wanted to understand, following the trajectory of a falling poem to its target,
one moment. i still want to. But poetry will not do it.
The poem, released, fails downward, detonates, scatters its staccato shrapnel syllables
      of meaning
but cannot devastate the mindscape of that moment into revelation, flay it bare unto
      my understanding.
Poetry is not destructive. Instead, the syllables recoil, fly backward from the moment,
back to before the bomb, before the atom split, before the first lie, back into
an awkward poem, a bomb straining to unexplode, its bulbous dart trying to deform itself
into a perfect globe, a sphere higher than i's can see, falling upward, back into
dimensions of unimaginable being where I-magination coheres indestructible atoms
      of true language into poems,
while here, shadows of fleeing words are caught, scorched onto the thin rice paper
      parchment of our lives.

API'S INTRAVIEW

They think
i talks funny.
They do not know.

They ask:
"Are you happy?"
i does not know.

"Well, what do you
want to be?"
i answers: "Api."

They smile, say:
"So do we."
And I laugh. Silently.

IN SINCERITY

And what else is there to write of
but my insincerity?
It's the reason in the first place
i have nothing else to write of
but my insincerity.

i'd describe a blackbird flying, ⋁—,
but i'd have to really see.
And true seeing needs a whole life
while this half-life that i lie in
is an insincerity.

Usual conflicts, contacts, conversations
i cannot take seriously.
Meetings, routines, life's assignments –
all a con, they're just evasions
of my insincerity.

And composing jaunty verses
on a deadly malady
is a sign that it is worsening.
Each of these words is a curse, is
sick with insincerity.

i went
from citizen
to spy
to double agent
one to three
discovering
my true element
in secrecy

in Rome, Roman
at home only
human, only
a self alone
always i act
from indirectives
cryptic lines
coded in tone

double agent, who
am i on behalf of,
half of? what
do i halve?
us? them? me?
no one
I make a whole
larger than country

ALTHOUGH THEY STRAIN

Words cannot hold the sorrow of the body of this world although they strain,
stretch thin, distorting into blisters as they try to hold it in
themselves, to keep the sickness of the world's anguished ages from breaking
through the skin of our afflicted lives, seeping out of our sored hands
raised above the bare heads of our children whom we try to bless.
Words swell, split, rupture their very meanings as they try
again, always again, to heal it in, to contain the origin of the sorrow,
how – absurdly – we turn so easily away from light, following
our attenuated shadows slipping over drying grass until an abrupt chasm,
until the full dark lips of an abyss which sips down finally into itself the sorrow,
not of the world, no, but of yourself at the unending sorrow of the world
which breaks through these now bleeding words that cannot heal or hold it in.

BIRD

(for Dennis Scott)

A poem has left its traces
in a thicket of a wild dark region of the mind,
the tip of a branch quivering still
from where the poem, alighting a moment, lifted away
suddenly, hearing a poet poaching.
           In that clearing to your left, a rustling of syllables,
close? distant? indistinct, stops when you stop
and listen: you do not hear the poem. It hears you.
The silence is the sound
of the poem listening.
           The poet starts again, approaching
a vined fall of tendrils trembling like nerved ganglia,
a fibrillating veil across a pathway in a last light.
He parts it, he is touched, he starts again, he enters
the thick felt darkness of the mind's wild
and the roar-grunt-chatter-wail-screech-howling of that interior
shrends at the air, straining to shock the skull open, to strike the poet
deaf unto himself.
           Under the flailing of your hundred voices, you hunch
in, inner, deep, going   to where all sounds,
even the light hush of anticipation,
dim to a silence without weight.
And that is where – sometimes – the bird
will somehow print its cries on air, will sing
its darkbright songs towards you from the parted leaves.

LAFWA POÈM-LA

Mwen di:
Kwik —
Pèsonn pa di *Kwak.*
Mwen hélé:
Tim-tim —
M'a tann anyen.
Mwen gadé —
Tout moun chapé,
kité mwen la mwen yonn.
Pa té ni pèsonn pèsonn pèsonn.
Ek an vwa ka chanté:
Manman-ou pa la
Papa-ou pa la
Sésé-ou pa la
Fwè-ou pa la
Tout moun alé… Mé
mwen fèt pa kò-mwen yonn,
kay mò pa kò-mwen yonn,
sé initil pléwé.

Alò, mwen doubout an mitan lavi-mwen,
gadé tout oliwon,
gadé anho, gadé anba…
Awa…
Yon sèl bagay mwen wè
sé ti poèm sala.
Mwen di an tjè-mwen:
Si sé sa, sé sa.
Mwen pwan kouway, mwen hélé:
Kwiiiiiiiiiiiiiiiiiiiiiiiiiiiiiiiiiiiiiiiiiiiiiiiiiiiiiiiiiiiiik!
Poèm-la wéponn:
Kwak!
Ek sé kon sa
mwen koumansé listwa.

POETRY FAITH

(Lafwa poèm-la — translation)

i call out:
Kweek
nobody answer *Kwak*
i bawl out:
Tim-tim
And i hear what?
Nothing.
i look all 'bout —
all run, give me their back.
Leave me right there, me one.
Not a single soul around.
And a voice, flinging this song:
your mother — gone
your father — gone
your sister — gone
your brother — gone
Gone — everyone.
But then, i born — alone.
And when i die — alone.
It make no sense to moan.

So i stand up my self right
in the middle o' me life
and look all round
look up, look down —
Awah…
One single thing i see —
this poem here, so small.
In the deep part of me
my voice come make my mind
say *If a so, a so*
Then i take heart, i call,
long, high:
Kweeeeeeeeeeeeeeeeeeeeeeeeeeeeeeeeeeeeeeeeeeeeeek!

i hear the poem, answering, cry
Kwak
A so
I-story start.

SONG FOR A MUSE

Come on a wave of a wind
My windows spread wide
Like arms to embrace
Will fold close when you stand inside
My feelings unskinned
Your hands on my face

Come on a wave of a wind
As seering as sun
Emblazoning trees
Unnoticed by all but the one
Calling you from within
Deep, where he sees

Through the mind's windows you come
With enbrightening eyes
Your wild hair unfurled
You strip my worn words of disguise
I am naked, blessedly dumb
Then you redress my world

TRIALECTICS AND THE PROBLEMATIC OF THE FORMULAIC PARADIGM/ PARADIGMATIC FORMULA(E) IN THE POETRY OF... WELL, WHOEVER...

Felt i should write something poetic.
Not great verse necessarily, just
nifty – so definitely not an epic.
Felt i should write something poetic.
And i thought: Well, why not trioletic?
So there. Need not be dissed or discussed.
Felt i should write something poetic.
Not great verse necessarily, just...

WRITING

He slits his wrist, the ink drips out
black on the white sheets, gouts
of dark blood stippling uncertainly
into what looks like a line, unfinished...
then, drip by drip, another line
blooding the sheet, seeping in to word
something – not there yet. He slits again
through artery, beyond art. There. Something
beyond the marks the ink makes on the sheet
will stain deeper than black on white
will stay, will say, will write
himself indelible into meaning.

TO WORD

Begin the day
wanting a communioning of Word and you, your head bowed
toward the page of empty lines, the spaces white in expectancy.
Wait. With the pen poised over the almost nothing
that is all   wait   without reason
watching the narrowing width between the pen's tip
and the line it aches toward.
Their touch, when they first meet, will be a point
so swift, evanescent, you may miss it.
It may vanish and, with it, you
into the loops and swirls, the strokes and criss-crosses of words
twisting all ways to lift themselves from and falling back onto
the empty lines. And you, so wanting Word, will then be language-lost.
Now squint back through the moment of the last time this happened
and wait in the awareness of again, your head bowed
lower, so close you can see this time the shadow of the pen.
Wait   beyond reason   before the quirk where all breaks into language
unto the point at which Word first will manifest.
As the pen lowers toward the shadow of the pen,
substantial in transcursion to the insubstantial,
you want to think. *How can they —*

O

Your lips, bud-opening into utterance, speak
the original syllable of all acknowledging
and Word is suffering itself into the empty lines
between the pen and shadow of the pen,
transgressing, fulfilling them with words.

CATACOMB

Dim in the afternoon fluorescent glare of the mundane recurring daze,
a single flame, suspended in an auric silence, flickers at you to follow
and leads you down into a catacomb below the shopping blocks, the city's trafficking.
There, in a grotto illuminant with a gold light impossible from that one flame,
you see rock paintings of a life you recognize but cannot remember having lived,
far less your having painted it – though who else could have known it well enough?
The tongue of flame that silently called you to this journey is invisible now
but in your mouth a heat, the chafe of words warming, wanting to speak, to say
to the busily dead and dying in the maze of streets-offices-stores above this place:
"Stop! Wait! Look for the flame!" But, returning to the white blare of the weak days,
the flame pales into neon, the incandescent words cool, contract, harden inside
        your mouth.
And yet once more you spit into your hands the luminous black stones of a poem,
strike them against each other, watching for sparks, waiting to quick a flame
to speak a lighted way out of the blindeadening maze down to the limned catacomb.

ADVICE TO A YOUNG POET

"What is poetry which does not save nations or people?" – *Czselaw Milosz*

Ask the question.
Not once but forty-nine times.
And, perhaps at the fiftieth,
you will make an answer.
Or perhaps not. Then
ask it again. This time
till seventy times seven. Ask
as you open the door
of every book of poems that you enter.
Ask it of every poem,
regardless of how beautiful,
that whispers: "Lie with me."
Do not spare your newborn.
If the first cry, first line
is not a wailing for an answer,
abandon it. As for the stillborn,
turn the next blank white sheet over,
shroud it. Ask the clamouring procession
of all the poems of the ages –
each measured, white-haired epic,
every flouncing free verse debutante –
to state their names, where they have come from
and what their business is with you.
You live in the caesura of our times,
the sound of nations, persons, breaking around you.
If poetry can only save itself,
then who will hear it after it has fled
from the nations and the people that it could not save
even a remnant of for a remembering?

SILVERFISH

Among the ordering furrows of print, you notice one day, casually, a hole
barely worth noticing on the page, whose words you turn over then go on
to the next. You are following the lines and they are leading you
on at first to the right, then, at the margin – invisible, unalterable –
back left, almost to exactly where you'd started but this time further of course
down. Then your left eye notices, between the penultimate and ultimate line,
the hole again, just as you are about to move up to another plot of cultivated rows.
When is it you notice that the hole is always there, that it is widening, lengthening
to a ditch, that bits of gnawed words are crumbling already into it?
Hard to pinpoint afterward on which page, reading a riddled text, you glimpsed
the silverfish, swifter than thought, wriggling through memories, theories, speculations.
But you knew then: something that does not follow edictatorial lines,
that evades ruts, that slips through the defiles, the very notion, of authority
will always undermine every attempt to fit words into ranks, keep them between margins.
The silverfish, burrowing unseen far down into the pages of our canonical texts,
underminds our cultivated fields of history, science's self-explanations, even literature.
A worm eats the ruled words of empires: the shouts, groans, proclamations, battle cries
are hushed into the susurration of the silverfish whispering through closed pages
the secret all empires must suppress, in order, to metastasize into empires:
that the I-magination lives beyond our ordering and is our ordering.
And a true poem is a glimpsed oblique track opened by the strenuous silver writhing
    of a poet
riddling a living way through dying language, creating a whole, hoping we fall, mindful,
    into it.

DISTANCE

No distance as long as a dim hospital corridor when,
coming to the end of it, before turning left, you do not know
if the door you walk to will be open
if the bed within will now be empty, stripped
if the quick, clipped phone call, "Come now", an hour ago
was an hour, half an hour, half of that, a minute, half a minute
late   No distance as long. Yet
you would prefer every remaining moment
of however many years of however long a life you have left
to be walking, walking this corridor, not coming to the end

NOVEMBER

Not that often, but far more often than i would have wanted to,
this year i have deleted numbers, email addresses, names
of those who are beyond the reach of phone calls, computer messages, letters
and the grasping of my voice whether i howl or whisper.
Last day of the month, almost 11:30, i lift the calendar's penultimate page
as a man might lift the trapdoor to the cellar in a crumbling house
where every room that he has opened so far
would have been better left shut.
It has been a year in which death was the constant weather,
lives slipping into shadow under an overcast of grey terminal conditions,
a drearying intermittent drizzle of sad illnesses,
then the long threatened rain hurling in with an obliterating blur.
i hold the page. One whole month before this year ends.
More rain. More contacts to delete.
i wish i could delete the past eleven months.
i hold November still, staring at numbers that begin to blur.
i drop the page. i want to shut the year closed.

FOUR POEMS TO A CROSSING

i

the mystery
of the infinite whirl
that is the present moment
self-spinning inward, stirring an inner life
spiralling outward into our sight, sound, touch, the senses,
existing, beyond all explication, in the very nature of existence,
cleaving the constructs of intellect, although not wholly, into mystery

ii
Schematically, precisely, the intellect aims to explicate preferably all
of the behaviour of each individual as the inevitable construct
of psycho-social forces entering through the aperture
of each event that he/she meets each day
and personalizing into actions
but – it meets a gap
a mystery

iii
Schematically, precisely, the intellect aims to explicate preferably all
of the behaviour of each individual as the inevitable construct
of psycho-social forces entering through the aperture
of each event that he/she meets each day
and personalizing into actions
but – it meets a gap
a mystery
the mystery
of the infinite whirl
that is the present moment
self-spinning inward, stirring an inner life
spiralling outward into our sight, sound, touch, the senses,
existing, beyond all explication, in the very nature of existence,
cleaving the constructs of intellect, although not wholly, into mystery

iv

Schematically, precisely, the intellect aims to explicate preferably all   *the mystery*
of the behaviour of each individual as the inevitable construct   *of the infinite whirl*
of psycho-social forces entering through the aperture   *that is the present moment*
of each event that he/she meets each day   *self-spinning inward, stirring an inner life*
and personalizing into actions   *spiralling outward into our sight, sound, touch, the senses,*
but – it meets a gap   *existing, beyond all explication, in the very nature of existence,*
a mystery   *cleaving the constructs of intellect, although not holy, into mystery*

STREAMS

two streams
one on the ground
one underground
flow differently

one sparkling
garrulous, shallow
one deep, quiet, slow
glimpsed – if – in dreams

they don't go
the same places
one trills on surfaces
one broods, in darkling

one goes sere
under harsh, hot sky
one flows, never dry
clear, liminal, below

"......."

i wake and slip into a deeper dream,
so deep, so real, that i believe i am awake, adrift among the drifting,
talking our selves to sleep and walking in the worlds our words make,
handling the hasty fragments of infinity our pincers of perception snip
out of the whole, so that we say: "tree" "sky" "sea"...
Somnambulant, speaking a split, slurred language that we splice for meaning,
we lull our selves, thinking that we are so awake, even insomniac,
we have to count the sheep of endless flocks of words,
our blurred-staring eyes covered by their soft wool as they softly leap
into our field of vision, crowding in there until we sleep
and in our sleep we walk a world where all the things we see,
and we who see, are in inverted comas

"TREE"
(for Ayo)

in the moment before "tree"
is trapped within inverted comas of perception
I see
that it is not
only a tree, although it is
only a tree the eye can see

in the moment unbeginning and unending
no thing can be
and the "tree" the eye is seeing
is the being of the All, momently
the I
seeing Itself
treeing

PATH
(for Mervyn Morris)

Where faith
Despair must be
Shaping each other
Naturally

Sudden chasm
And you know
Lost in wilderness
Where to go

Winding edge
Of precipice
A path
You cannot miss

SEWING

Every morning, pick up the torn bits of cloth, lift them
up from wherever they fell, ripped softly during sleep and scattered.
Accept, as best you can, that the selfhood is a patchwork thing,
always fraying, made from tatters, swatches
of a rainbow swathe of whole cloth that unrolled to earth
and that you must sew,
make raggedy, uneven seams with the thin thread of will
that frays too, that trembles uncertainly before the needle's single I.
Sew anyway. What else is worth doing?
Sew. Make the quilt.

WAYS

They were walking – he, left   she, right – on a winding path below the speckled foliage,
he speaking quietly, she listening easily, so neither saw or heard at first
when the ground cracked and a long fissure wavered ahead of them along the path

and they began to walk on either side of it on parallel tracks while he kept talking
just a bit more loudly and she strained – but just a bit – to listen, and at first
they did not notice since they were still walking – he | she – in the same direction

and even when their parallel companionable journeys brought them finally
to where the track split, forking into a serpent's tongue, transforming the pathway's
        single I
into a Y... they paused only slightly, looking ahead, each one, into the distance,

then continued – he, crossing to right   she, crossing to left – both barely noticing
he was speaking more loudly, she was listening harder, and both straining now,
he, looking at her over his left shoulder   she, looking at him over her right

and how long they misconversed like that, neither remembered afterward, only that
this was the only way that they could keep with insight of each other
although his voice to her, her form to him, as they continued, became fainter

and they continued walking, neither seeing where his own\ /her own journey led
        because
each needed to keep looking at the other to feel oriented, and in truth it was easier
to see each other's path, and as their separate journeys widened into ways apart,

he began shouting with all he was worth but she could not hear him across the distance
and she bared herself till she was naked   but he could not see her across the distance
and they continued, they continue – shouting and unheard\ /naked and unseen – along
        their ways, cleft

and if they could, just once, look far enough into the distance, and just once, behind,
they'd see the way all led back to the Y... and they would find, again and yet beyond again,
their journey.

BLUE HYDRANGEAS

i have to listen to the earth again, i've been forgetting.
But that afternoon, i remembered. And i am still

following the purling of the mountain road up into country,
the city behind us wafting downward, or snagged at times in bush,
the road itself crack-toothed, weatherbeaten grey
like the occasional countryman gravely raising a hand as we pass
alongside the insouciant slant of the young bamboo fluttering,
slowing down as we veer inward from the road-edge where the blue mahoe
loom upward like the necks of dinosaurs from the deep ravines,
speeding again under the watchful gaze of pines – prim, watchful country schoolmistresses
with every reticent, stiff hair hair in place, each proper stance meticulous.
        Then, climbing another col, rounding the next corner, we travel deeper
into an earlier time, i have to say. It happens simply but
it's true: this land, which after rainfall chews down chunks of road
into its gorges and heaves its hawked-up sputa onto gouged asphalt,
does not know man. This fraying rag of road, those scattered chips of houses
and the two of us, more quiet now, are here on sufferance.
        Travelling upward still, into cold, sometimes landscape steps out of mist,
gesticulating, then shies away, shivering, hugging its foliage
tighter around brown rock softening to skin under the wrinkling of water.
        In this terrain, height calls to height
across far precipices muslined in rain, which even to look at
makes the ground drop suddenly under you one belly-lurching moment.
        Height calls to height.
But i have not said it yet, have still not spoken
of the presence. There
in the place of flowers where we, and everything, stopped.
When we left the jeep, it followed, timing its footsteps
into ours so as not to be heard, whispering underneath our words
to hide itself. But sometimes, in a pause of conversation,
after the sift of words, inside the falling silence,
another voice was fading.
        Height calling still to height.

In such terrain, there is the sound, there is the echo,
there is the moment after.
                    That afternoon, a sidelong sense
of inhabiting the moment when the echo was, unsure
of what i'd heard, of what was now, but glanced
by after-ripples of a sound just missed, always just missed.
                    And it is only now, writing to you,
i'm understanding finally why, of all that day of miracle,
what comes, what lives with me, is when i pointed to
a brilliantly sky-blue brooch of clustering petals, asking:
"What do you call these?"

                    And that was when
the angel, who had all afternoon been speaking
in the vocabulary of flowers, singing in the steep descant of cliff,
reading aloud a valley's open text of silence gilted with light,
spoke finally in our struggling language; and your voice,
a shade beyond normal, after a moment's hesitance,
not from uncertainty, but from a kind of waiting, said
(and i feel again the soft, delayed shock of the moment):
"Hydrangeas."

            That was when.

GLINT

It is seen, more often than not, in glimpses:
a glint through a never-before-noticed crack in a high wall
on your left as you, walking your too hurriedly usual way
and looking, as usual, straight ahead, realise – Oh! –
something just winked at you, light
broke through the wall a moment ago and left
this hair-thin wavering line (surely it wasn't there a moment ago?)
puzzling along at just eye-level all the rest of your way to
wherever it was you had originally intended to go
but which is less important now
than straining to see, into and past the crack,
what on the other side had winked peripherally at you –

then you give up, walking in slow attentivity, following the fault line
seeping alongside, widening too infinitesmally for sight to squint through but widening
to the corner where the wall has split
and you turn left from what you had been straining hard to see
into the seen, held in a beholding, opening from glimpse into envisioning
– trance – brief as a wink – then you are following again
the wrinkling transecting line through which, for a moment, split,
you saw it

LINES ON A SIDEWALK

Where the sidewalk splits, where grass cracks an unexpected gash across
      the concrete surface,
where the unseen black broil of earth seethes upward,
starting green fires flickering on these cemented urban ways, now fractured
there   a fault line of possibility where new breaks into knowing
and you sense your eyes warm wider open from, and to, a light
inciting you to, for the first time, yet again, see.
See: that no matter how, how much, how often, how long we slab the earth,
she will breach us, grab back her ground from our suave hands trying to smooth her over.
See: that underneath our feet she is convulsing – roots, rocks wrestling each other
in the dirt that worms blur through – in an unsounded, subterranean, aeonic gnash
      of elements.
See: that like the silent, unseen furying of the caterpillar struggling to beyond itself,
earth is a metamorphosis. And what she will finally become is hidden from us.
That wry quirk in the sidewalk that the grass has suddenly blazed from
(between one day and the next, it seems) has let through a momentary light, an insight:
a true civilisation builds a way of living
at the seaming fault between humanity's fulfillment and nature's.
And perhaps if all our ways were like old flagstone paths,
acknowledging the grass growing between our footsteps as well as the going of our feet,
we might eventually reach a different destination. But as things are now,
i think the sidewalk should remain cracked, for the quick green flames to flicker
their almost unnoticed light that – briefly, imperfectly – relumes another way.

ARCHIPELAGO

If you really see the Caribbean archipelago, you will see yourself,
the vivid scattered islands stirring to awakening in a sea of reverie and nightmare,
the goldening light lifting green foliage out of darkness into its illumination
and the surrounding blue immensity brooding an unknown creaturing of what can live
      only in depth

If you hear the Caribbean archipelago, you will hear it talking to you in tongues
of the original tribes of the Americas, Africa, Europe, Asia; you will hear quarrelling,
      then a blur
and you will hear the simultaneous translation of these languages into the first language,
the sea talking to itself because in the beginning and the end there is no other

If you truly see the Caribbean archipelago, it will become clear
how the fragmented, brittle arc of islands, resisting the onsurge of ocean, makes
      the sea the sea;
how the ocean, reaching around breached rock, trying to rejoin itself, makes
      islands islands;
how they both therefore define each other, how they refine your understanding of
      the selfhood
into an acceptance of the necessary oneness of the known and the unknown

If you can be the Caribbean archipelago, acknowledging that your littoral shape is
      never final,
that it shifts with your awareness that below the sublunary rise-and-ebb there is
      an undertow,
a contrary flow that draws you down, deepening to where the separate i-lands reach
beyond the scattered stones of their selves, growing down back into one bedrock, into
      the original
ground from which the sea, the ocean, the self-dismembered yet defining archipelago rise
      into their being,
if you can be this, be yond it, you will miracle into impossibility, you will see
how to be broken and yet whole.

ABOUT THE AUTHOR

Born in St. Lucia in 1952, he studied and lived in Jamaica in the 1970s, where he explored his talents as a poet, playwright and director. As a poet, his writing ranges across the continuum of language from Standard English to the varieties of Caribbean English and he has also written poems in Kweyol, his nation language. He works in traditional forms like the sonnet and villanelle as well as in so-called free verse and in forms influenced by rap and reggae. He has published five books of poetry, the latest being *Night Vision* (TriQuarterly Books, Northwestern University Press, 2005) and his poetry has appeared in various journals such as *The Greenfield Review*, *The Massachusetts Review* and in anthologies such as *Caribbean Poetry Now*, *Voiceprint*, *West Indian Poetry* and others. He has also edited *Confluence: Nine St. Lucian Poets*, *So Much Poetry in We People*, an anthology of performance poetry from the Eastern Caribbean, *This Poem-Worthy Place*, an anthology of poems from Bermuda, as well as student anthologies from creative writing students at the Sir Arthur Lewis Community College where he was a lecturer in literature and drama until 2007.

He has participated in poetry workshops by Derek Walcott and Mervyn Morris. He has himself designed and taught poetry workshops in various places such as Ty Newydd in Wales and the UWI Caribbean Writers Summer Workshop in Barbados.

He has performed his work in the Caribbean, Europe and America at events such as the Miami International Book Fair, the Medellin Poetry Festival, Calabash Literary Festival, Vibrations Caraibes, the Havana Book Fair among others. In 2007, he won the Bridget Jones Travel Award to travel to England to present his one-man dramatized poetry production, Kinky Blues, at the annual conference of the Society for Caribbean Studies. He has twice won the Literature prize in the Minvielle & Chastanet Fine Arts Awards, for many years the premier arts award scheme in St. Lucia. He has been the recipient of a James Michener Fellowship to study poetry and an OAS scholarship to study theatre.

He has also established himself as an innovative playwright and director, authoring eight plays, and directing scores of others, including his own *The Drum-Maker* (1976), *The Song of One* (1995) and *Triptych* (2000), all of which have been published in drama anthologies. In 1984, he co-founded the Lighthouse Theatre Company in St. Lucia, and has long been involved in all aspects of the dramatic arts on the island. He has toured with theatre productions in the Caribbean and the UK. At different times he has been involved as actor, director and administrator in Saint Lucia's contingents travelling to CARIFESTA. He is an original and continuing member of the syllabus panel for the Caribbean Examinations Council (CXC) Theatre Arts programme and serves as an external examiner.

In 2000, Kendel was awarded the St. Lucia Medal of Merit (Gold) for Contribution to the Arts. Recently retired from the Sir Arthur Lewis Community College, his present focus is to use his skills as a writer and dramatist to raise public awareness and contribute to active solutions of critical social issues.

ALSO BY KENDEL HIPPOLYTE

Birthright
ISBN: 9780948833939; pp. 124; pub. February 1997; price: £8.99.

The Heinemann Book of Caribbean Poetry described Kendel Hippolyte as "perhaps the outstanding Caribbean poet of his generation". Until now his poetry has only been available in anthologies and slim collections which have been little seen outside St. Lucia. *Birthright* reveals him as a poet who combines acute intelligence and passion, a barbed wit and lyrical tenderness.

He writes with satirical anger from the perspective of an island marginalised by the international money markets in a prophetic voice whose ancestry is Blake, Whitman and Lawrence, married to the contemporary influences of reggae, rastafarian word-play and a dread cosmology. He writes, too, with an acute control of formal structures, of sound, rhythm and rhyme – there are sonnets and even a villanelle – but like "Bunny Wailer flailing Apollyon with a single song", his poetry has "a deepdown spiritual chanting rising upfull-I". Whilst acknowledging a debt of influence and admiration to his fellow St. Lucian, Derek Walcott, Kendel Hippolyte's poetry has a direct force which is in the best sense a corrective to Walcott's tendency to romanticise the St. Lucian landscape and people.

Kwame Dawes writes: "It is clear that Hippolyte's social consciousness is subordinated to his fascination with words, with the poetics of language, and so in the end we are left with a sense of having taken a journey with a poet who loves the musicality of his words. His more overtly craft conscious neo-formalist pieces are deft, efficient and never strained. Villanelles, sonnets and interesting rhyming verse show his discipline and the quiet concentration of a poet who does not write for the rat race of the publishing world, but for himself. One gets the sense of a writer working in a laboratory patiently, waiting for the right image to come, and then placing it there only when it comes. This calm, this devotion is enviable for frenetic writers like myself who act as if there is a death wish on our heads or a promise of early passing. Our poetry, one suspects, suffers. Hippolyte shows no such anxiety and the result is verse of remarkable grace and beauty."